# Music
## Through Time
### CLARINET BOOK 3

## SELECTED AND EDITED BY
# Paul Harris

MUSIC DEPARTMENT

OXFORD
UNIVERSITY PRESS

# OXFORD
### UNIVERSITY PRESS

Great Clarendon Street, Oxford OX2 6DP, England
198 Madison Avenue, New York, NY 10016, USA

Oxford University Press is a department of the University of Oxford.
It furthers the University's aim of excellence in research, scholarship,
and education by publishing worldwide

Oxford is a registered trade mark of Oxford University Press
in the UK and in certain other countries

ISBN 0-19-357186-2   978-0-19-357186-0

Printed in Great Britain on acid-free paper by
Caligraving Ltd., Thetford, Norfolk.

All of the pieces in this collection are arranged
for clarinet and piano by Paul Harris

# Pavane for the Earl of Salisbury

*William Byrd*
(1542–1623)

The Italian scientist Galileo Galilei continued to develop the telescope, achieving up to thirty-two times magnification. He proved that the Milky Way was made up of stars and discovered many which were invisible to the naked eye. The newly translated King James Version of the Bible appeared; it would be the standard version for the next 300 years.

The pavane was a slow, stately dance, especially popular in the sixteenth and seventeenth centuries. This one was dedicated to Byrd's patron, the Earl of Salisbury.

# 1722
# March

*Johann Sebastian Bach*
(1685–1750)

Dutch explorers discovered Easter Island in the Pacific Ocean, famous for its massive stone statues which were carved by the sun-worshipping inhabitants some 200 years earlier. Archeologists still don't understand how they were erected.

This piece is taken from one of the collections of keyboard music that Bach made for his second wife, Anna Magdalena.

Printed in Great Britain
OXFORD UNIVERSITY PRESS, MUSIC DEPARTMENT, GREAT CLARENDON STREET, OXFORD OX2 6DP

*c.1730*
# Adagio

*Remo Giazotto–Tommaso Albinoni*
(1671–1750)

The Serpentine lake was built in London's Hyde Park and the following year an elegant house, No. 10 Downing Street, became the official residence of the Prime Minister of Great Britain.

Albinoni was a prolific Italian composer. He wrote over 200 operas, never (it is said) spending more than a week on each one! This adagio, his most popular work, was reconstructed from a manuscript fragment by the twentieth-century Italian musicologist Remo Giazotto.

America was in the midst of the Revolution to overthrow British control. Yorkshireman Joseph Bramah patented his water-closet—the forerunner of the modern lavatory—first designed for Queen Elizabeth I by the courtier Sir John Harrington in 1596.

The trio section of a minuet and trio was so-called because of the French practice of writing these sections in three-part harmony. By the end of the eighteenth century the custom had fallen out of use, but the 'trio' label stuck.

# 1778
# Minuet and Trio

## *Wolfgang Amadeus Mozart*
### (1756–91)

# 1802
# Melody

Atomic theory was introduced into chemistry by John Dalton, and gas lighting was first demonstrated in the UK. The first attempt was made to regulate factory working conditions to no more than twelve hours a day.

## Jean-Xavier Lefèvre
(1763–1829)

Lefèvre composed the first known sonatas for clarinet as well as a tutor, concertos, and many smaller pieces. He was also responsible for the sixth key to be added to the clarinet, the C#/G# key.

# 1805
# Grazioso

The British fleet defeated the French and Spanish navies at the battle of Trafalgar. The Admiral of the Fleet, Lord Nelson, was hit by gunfire and died in the arms of the officers of his flagship *Victory*.

## Frederic Blasius
(1758–1829)

Blasius played the clarinet, violin, and bassoon in addition to composing. His works include four concertos and a clarinet tutor.

A group of men called the 'Luddites' started smashing the new machines which were taking over the textile industry and putting them out of their jobs. They operated in great secrecy, and were followers of Ned Ludd, who came from Sherwood Forest and was seen as a new Robin Hood—a friend of the poor and weak.

This andante is the theme from the *Silvana Variations*, a set of variations written in an afternoon and first performed that same evening by the clarinet virtuoso Heinrich Bärmann, with the composer at the piano.

*1811*
# Andante con moto

*Carl Maria von Weber*
(1786–1826)

## 1815
# Waltz

After seeing some children playing with long, hollow pieces of wood, the French doctor René Laennec invented a simple stethoscope to listen to heart-beats. In Britain, meanwhile, the Apothecaries Act was passed, making it illegal for self-styled 'doctors' with no qualifications to practice medicine.

One of Schubert's favourite haunts was a Viennese coffee-house frequented by Beethoven. The timid Schubert would sit gazing reverently at the figure of the great man alone in the corner.

### *Franz Schubert*
(1797–1828)

## 1828
# Melody

The Duke of Wellington—known for his famous boots—became Prime Minister of Great Britain. Sir Charles Wheatstone perfected his design for the concertina, at one time so popular in high society that it had several professors of virtuoso ability.

Boieldieu is known mainly as an opera composer, but he also wrote chamber music and piano pieces. He was a brilliant pianist, and taught at the Paris Conservatoire.

### *Adrien Boieldieu*
(1775–1834)

# Music Through Time

## CLARINET BOOK 3
## PIANO ACCOMPANIMENTS

### CONTENTS

SELECTED AND EDITED BY
## Paul Harris

# 1611
# Pavane for the Earl of Salisbury

*William Byrd*
(1542–1623)

The Italian scientist Galileo Galilei continued to develop the telescope, achieving up to thirty-two times magnification. He proved that the Milky Way was made up of stars and discovered many which were invisible to the naked eye. The newly translated King James Version of the Bible appeared; it would be the standard version for the next 300 years.

The pavane was a slow, stately dance, especially popular in the sixteenth and seventeenth centuries. This one was dedicated to Byrd's patron, the Earl of Salisbury.

Dutch explorers discovered Easter Island in the Pacific Ocean, famous for its massive stone statues which were carved by the sun-worshipping inhabitants some 200 years earlier. Archeologists still don't understand how they were erected.

This piece is taken from one of the collections of keyboard music that Bach made for his second wife, Anna Magdalena.

*Johann Sebastian Bach*
(1685–1750)

*c.1730*
# Adagio

*Remo Giazotto–Tommaso Albinoni*
(1671–1750)

The Serpentine lake was built in London's Hyde Park and the following year an elegant house, No. 10 Downing Street, became the official residence of the Prime Minister of Great Britain.

Albinoni was a prolific Italian composer. He wrote over 200 operas, never (it is said) spending more than a week on each one! This adagio, his most popular work, was reconstructed from a manuscript fragment by the twentieth-century Italian musicologist Remo Giazotto.

## 1778
# Minuet and Trio

America was in the midst of the Revolution to overthrow British control. Yorkshireman Joseph Bramah patented his water-closet—the forerunner of the modern lavatory— first designed  for Queen Elizabeth I by the courtier Sir John Harrington in 1596.

The trio section of a minuet and trio was so-called because of the French practice of writing these sections in three-part harmony. By the end of the eighteenth century the custom had fallen out of use, but the 'trio' label stuck.

*Wolfgang Amadeus Mozart*
(1756–91)

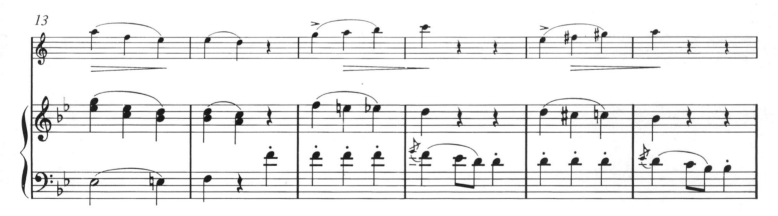

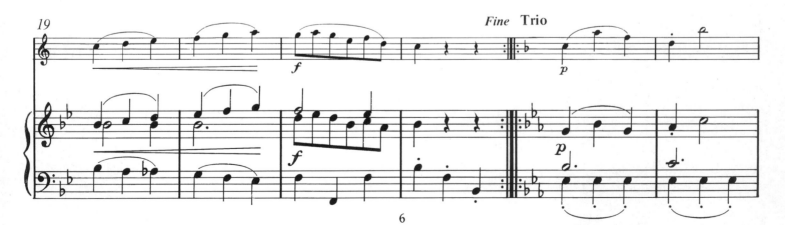

# 1802
# Melody

*Jean-Xavier Lefèvre*
(1763–1829)

Atomic theory was introduced into chemistry by John Dalton, and gas lighting was first demonstrated in the UK. The first attempt was made to regulate factory working conditions to no more than twelve hours a day.

Lefèvre composed the first known sonatas for clarinet as well as a tutor, concertos, and many smaller pieces. He was also responsible for the sixth key to be added to the clarinet, the C#/G# key.

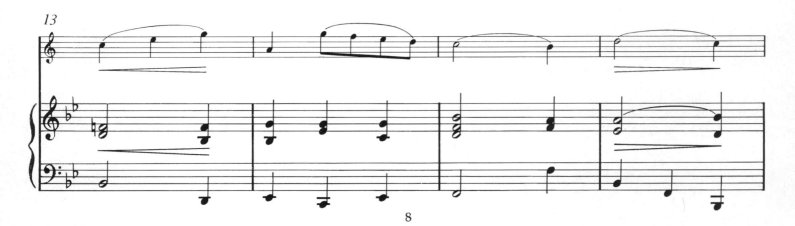

# 1805
# Grazioso

*Frederic Blasius*
(1758–1829)

The British fleet defeated the French and Spanish navies at the battle of Trafalgar. The Admiral of the Fleet, Lord Nelson, was hit by gunfire and died in the arms of the officers of his flagship *Victory*.

Blasius played the clarinet, violin, and bassoon in addition to composing. His works include four concertos and a clarinet tutor.

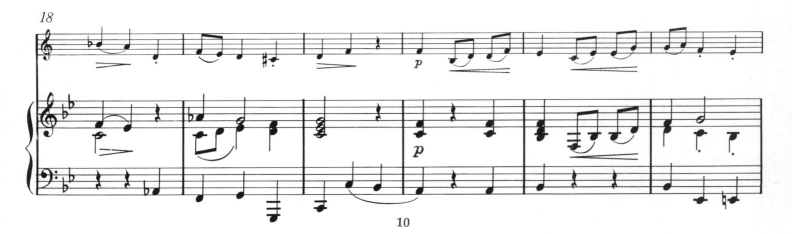

# 1811
# Andante con moto

*Carl Maria von Weber*
(1786–1826)

A group of men called the 'Luddites' started smashing the new machines which were taking over the textile industry and putting them out of their jobs. They operated in great secrecy, and were followers of Ned Ludd, who came from Sherwood Forest and was seen as a new Robin Hood—a friend of the poor and weak.

This andante is the theme from the *Silvana Variations*, a set of variations written in an afternoon and first performed that same evening by the clarinet virtuoso Heinrich Bärmann, with the composer at the piano.

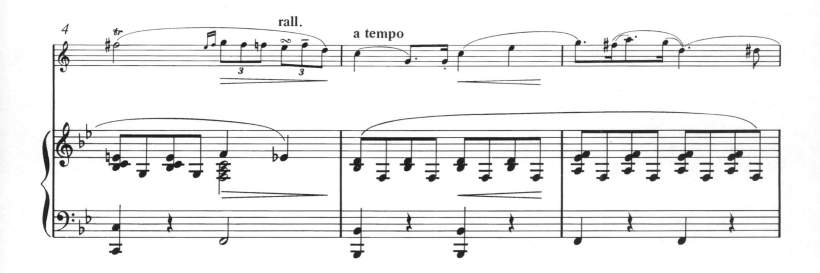

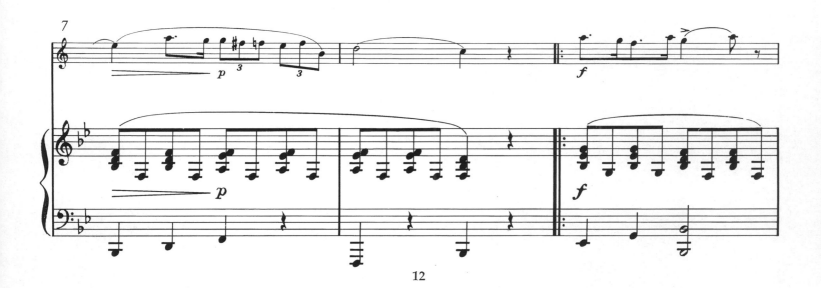

# 1815
# Waltz

*Franz Schubert*
(1797–1828)

After seeing some children playing with long, hollow pieces of wood, the French doctor René Laennec invented a simple stethoscope to listen to heart-beats. In Britain, meanwhile, the Apothecaries Act was passed, making it illegal for self-styled 'doctors' with no qualifications to practice medicine.

One of Schubert's favourite haunts was a Viennese coffee-house frequented by Beethoven. The timid Schubert would sit gazing reverently at the figure of the great man alone in the corner.

# 1828
# Melody

*Adrien Boieldieu*
(1775–1834)

The Duke of Wellington—known for his famous boots—became Prime Minister of Great Britain. Sir Charles Wheatstone perfected his design for the concertina, at one time so popular in high society that it had several professors of virtuoso ability.

Boieldieu is known mainly as an opera composer, but he also wrote chamber music and piano pieces. He was a brilliant pianist, and taught at the Paris Conservatoire.

In Britain, Isaac Pitman invented his 'Stenographic Sound Hand', a shorthand system based on phonetics which enabled writing of up to fifty words per minute. In the USA, Samuel Morse developed his code based on dots and dashes, which would revolutionize world communication.

Berr was an important clarinet player. He composed many works for the instrument and wrote a well-known tutor.

# Melody

*Frédéric Berr*
(1794–1838)

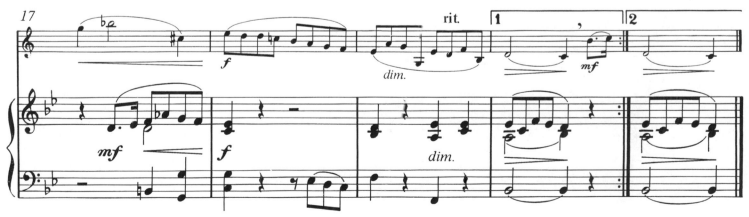

# 1865
# Après un rêve

*Gabriel Fauré*
(1845–1924)

Oxford mathematician Charles Dodson wrote *Alice's Adventures in Wonderland* under the name of Lewis Carroll. The American Civil War ended on 9 April when the Southern Confederate forces surrendered to the Northern Union. Six days later, Abraham Lincoln was assassinated in a Washington theatre by John Wilkes Booth, a failed actor.

Fauré, who was an organist, composer, and teacher, was appointed director of the Paris Conservatoire in 1905. This piece, his most popular song, has been arranged for many instruments.

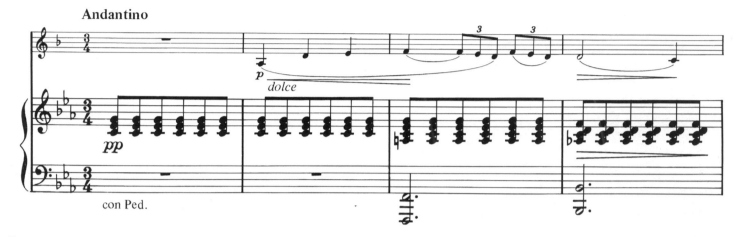

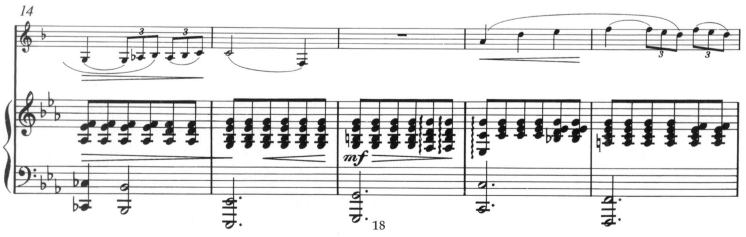

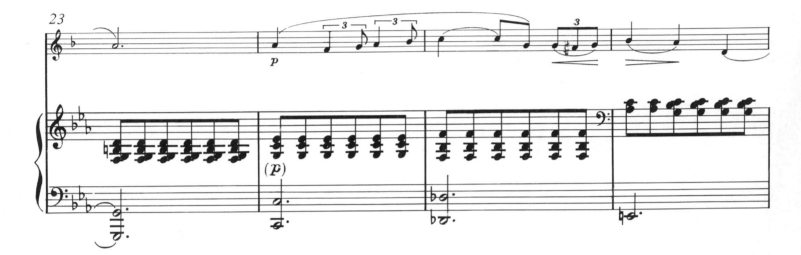

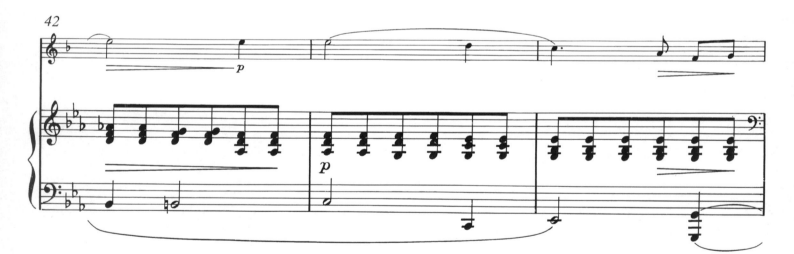

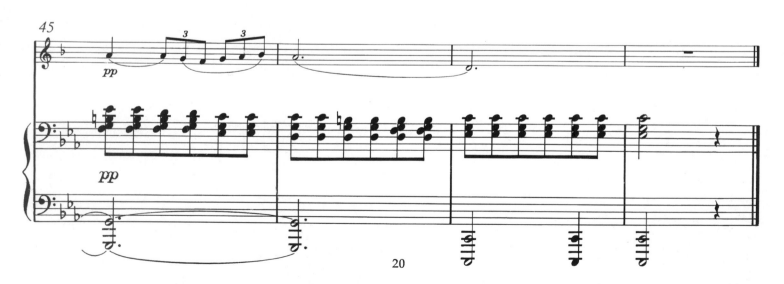

In the year of her Jubilee, Queen Victoria met the famous American gunslinger Annie Oakley. Oakley, who later became the subject of the musical *Annie Get Your Gun*, could shoot a playing card in half from thirty paces.

The hornpipe was a popular sailors' dance. This one appears in Gilbert and Sullivan's comic opera Ruddigore.

*Arthur Sullivan*

(1842–1900)

# 1892
# Allegretto

*Edward Elgar*
(1857–1934)

Exciting developments in the world of technology: the American William Burroughs patented the first practical calculator that could print its calculations, the British scientist James Dewar invented the vacuum flask, and the Frenchman Monsieur Hennebique invented reinforced concrete. In a year's time, Whitcombe Judson, a Chicago engineer, will patent the zip fastener!

Sir Edward Elgar was one of England's greatest composers, and wrote this little allegretto as one of a set of six easy violin pieces for his niece.

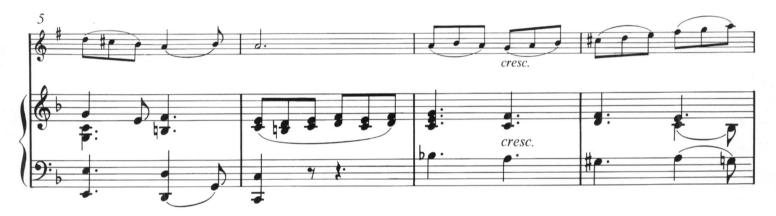

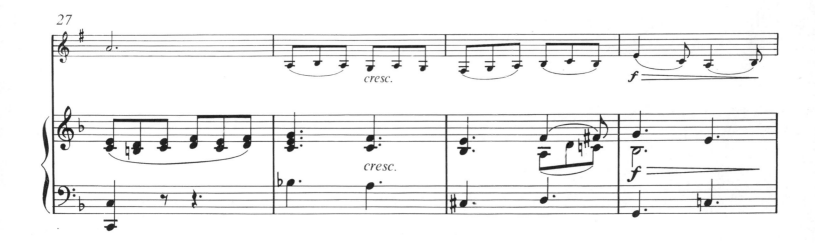

## *1893*
# Romance

Karl Benz in Germany and Henry Ford in the USA built their first motor cars.
Rudyard Kipling wrote *The Jungle Book* and in Chicago the first self-service
restaurant was opened. Alexander Graham Bell made the first long-distance
telephone call, from Chicago (not the restaurant!) to New York.

Edward German studied at the Royal Academy of Music in London and
eventually became musical director of the Globe Theatre. One of his best-known
works is the operetta *Merrie England*.

*Edward German*

(1863–1936)

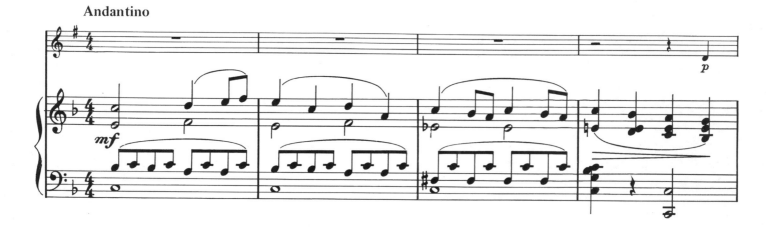

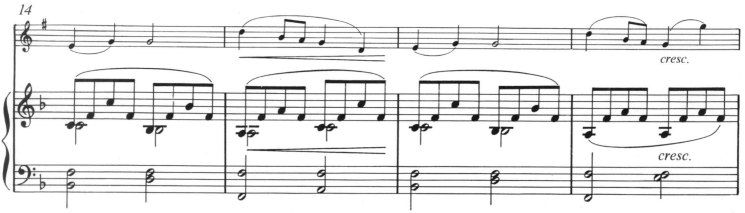

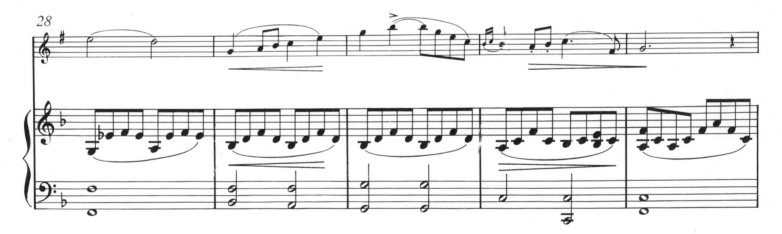

## 1901
# The Easy Winners

*Scott Joplin*
(1868–1917)

Queen Victoria died after a reign of 63 years, aged 81. The first effective vacuum cleaner (it sucked, rather than blew) was invented by Hubert Booth. Marconi succeeded in sending the first transatlantic radio signal, the first motor-driven bicycle was made, and the first Nobel prizes were awarded.

Scott Joplin popularized the piano rag with his *Maple Leaf Rag*, initially turned down for publication as being too difficult. He always said that his rags should not be played too fast.

# 1908
# Pavane of the Sleeping Beauty

*Maurice Ravel*

(1875–1937)

The Wright brothers patented their 'flying machine'. In China, the two-year-old Emperor Puyi succeeded the 'Old Buddha', the Empress Dowager, to the Imperial throne. She had died, aged 73, from eating too enormous a helping of her favourite pudding—crab-apples and cream!

A pavane is a slow dance. This one comes from Ravel's ballet *Mother Goose*, based on a fairy-tale by Pericault.

In France, some children accidentally discovered the Lascaux Cave paintings, dating from 20,000 years earlier. Walt Disney's cartoon Fantasia, which features many great pieces of music, was released. Howard Florey saved many lives by developing the antibiotic penicillin in large quantities—essential in wartime.

Although Walton was a cathedral chorister, he had very little formal musical training. He's perhaps best known for his coronation march *Crown Imperial*, a true successor to Elgar's 'Pomp and Circumstance' marches.

*William Walton*
(1902–83)

# 1990
# Ghoulish

*Paul Harris*
(1957–   )

Try to create a dramatic, spooky
atmosphere when you play this piece.

The texture is very sparse, and the
changes of dynamic should lend an
air of mystery to this evocative
character piece.

**In a sinister manner**

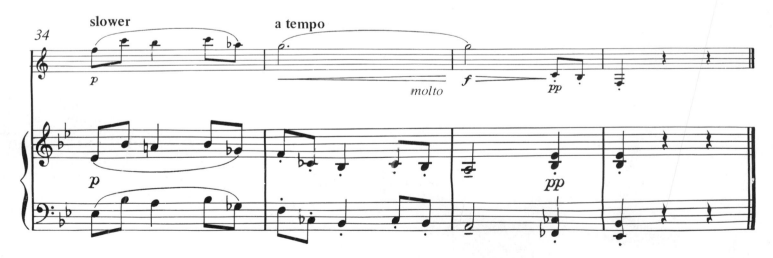

31

Printed in Great Britain by Caligraving Ltd, Thetford, Norfolk.

In Britain, Isaac Pitman invented his 'Stenographic Sound Hand', a shorthand system based on phonetics which enabled writing of up to fifty words per minute. In the USA, Samuel Morse developed his code based on dots and dashes, which would revolutionize world communication.

Berr was an important clarinet player. He composed many works for the instrument and wrote a well-known tutor.

## 1836
# Melody

*Frédéric Berr*
(1794–1838)

# 1865
# Après un rêve

## Gabriel Fauré
(1845–1924)

Oxford mathematician Charles Dodson wrote *Alice's Adventures in Wonderland* under the name of Lewis Carroll. The American Civil War ended on 9 April when the Southern Confederate forces surrendered to the Northern Union. Six days later, Abraham Lincoln was assassinated in a Washington theatre by John Wilkes Booth, a failed actor.

Fauré, who was an organist, composer, and teacher, was appointed director of the Paris Conservatoire in 1905. This piece, his most popular song, has been arranged for many instruments.

In the year of her Jubilee, Queen Victoria met the famous American gunslinger Annie Oakley. Oakley, who later became the subject of the musical *Annie Get Your Gun*, could shoot a playing card in half from thirty paces.

The hornpipe was a popular sailors' dance. This one appears in Gilbert and Sullivan's comic opera Ruddigore.

*1887*
# Hornpipe

## *Arthur Sullivan*
### (1842–1900)

Exciting developments in the world of technology: the American William Burroughs patented the first practical calculator that could print its calculations, the British scientist James Dewar invented the vacuum flask, and the Frenchman Monsieur Hennebique invented reinforced concrete. In a year's time, Whitcombe Judson, a Chicago engineer, will patent the zip fastener!

Sir Edward Elgar was one of England's greatest composers, and wrote this little allegretto as one of a set of six easy violin pieces for his niece.

*1892*
# Allegretto

## *Edward Elgar*
### (1857–1934)

## 1893
# Romance

*Edward German*

(1863–1936)

Karl Benz in Germany and Henry Ford in the USA built their first motor cars. Rudyard Kipling wrote *The Jungle Book* and in Chicago the first self-service restaurant was opened. Alexander Graham Bell made the first long-distance telephone call, from Chicago (not the restaurant!) to New York.

Edward German studied at the Royal Academy of Music in London and eventually became musical director of the Globe Theatre. One of his best-known works is the operetta *Merrie England*.

Queen Victoria died after a reign of 63 years, aged 81. The first effective vacuum cleaner (it sucked, rather than blew) was invented by Hubert Booth. Marconi succeeded in sending the first transatlantic radio signal, the first motor-driven bicycle was made, and the first Nobel prizes were awarded.

Scott Joplin popularized the piano rag with his *Maple Leaf Rag*, initially turned down for publication as being too difficult. He always said that his rags should not be played too fast.

# The Easy Winners

*Scott Joplin*
(1868–1917)

## 1908
# Pavane of the Sleeping Beauty
*Maurice Ravel*
(1875–1937)

The Wright brothers patented their 'flying machine'. In China, the two-year-old Emperor Puyi succeeded the 'Old Buddha', the Empress Dowager, to the Imperial throne. She had died, aged 73, from eating too enormous a helping of her favourite pudding—crab-apples and cream!

A pavane is a slow dance. This one comes from Ravel's ballet *Mother Goose*, based on a fairy-tale by Pericault.

## 1940
# The Silent Lake

*William Walton*
(1902–83)

In France, some children accidentally discovered the Lascaux Cave paintings, dating from 20,000 years earlier. Walt Disney's cartoon Fantasia, which features many great pieces of music, was released. Howard Florey saved many lives by developing the antibiotic penicillin in large quantities—essential in wartime.

Although Walton was a cathedral chorister, he had very little formal musical training. He's perhaps best known for his coronation march *Crown Imperial*, a true successor to Elgar's 'Pomp and Circumstance' marches.

14

Try to create a dramatic, spooky
atmosphere when you play this piece.

The texture is very sparse, and the
changes of dynamic should lend an
air of mystery to this evocative
character piece.

*1990*
# Ghoulish

*Paul Harris*
(1957-  )